AND ON THE EIGHTH DAY GOD MADE AMERICA

Simon Bond
TOTALLY
U.S.

Salem House

Published by
Salem House Publishers
462 Boston Street
Topsfield, MA 01983
Copyright © Polycarp Ltd 1988

Photoset and Printed in the United States

Library of Congress Catalog Card Number:
88-80954

ISBN 0-88162-368-7

Versions of 'State of the Nation' and 'The Mormon Tabernacle Trio'
originally appeared in *The New Yorker*.

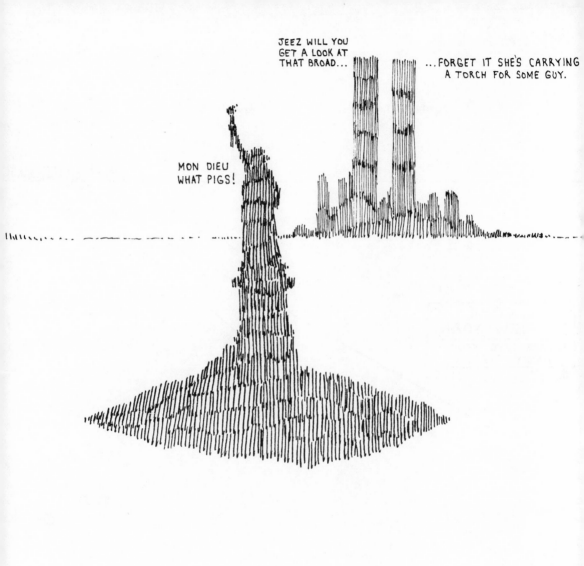

WELCOME
TO NEW YORK
PLEASE HAVE YOUR
MONEY READY

'Belwood, the market's down . . . wake me in a week.'

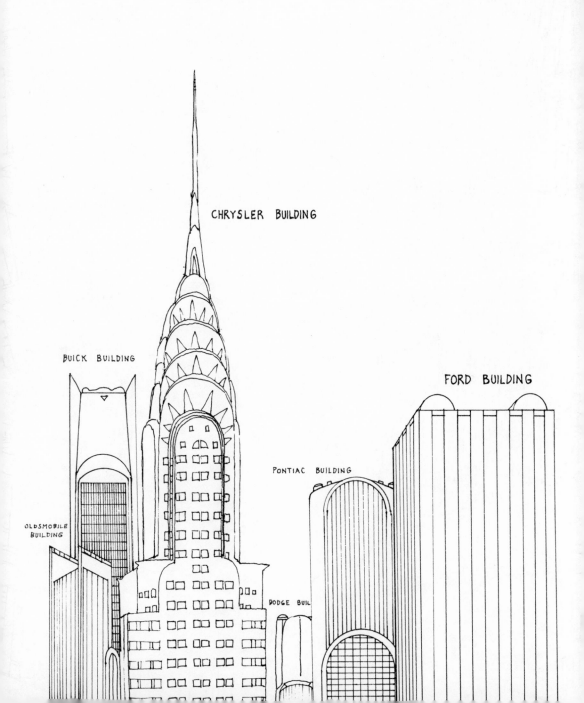

CONEY ISLAND 1491

THE BREAKFAST MEETING
*Can you spot the deliberate mistake?

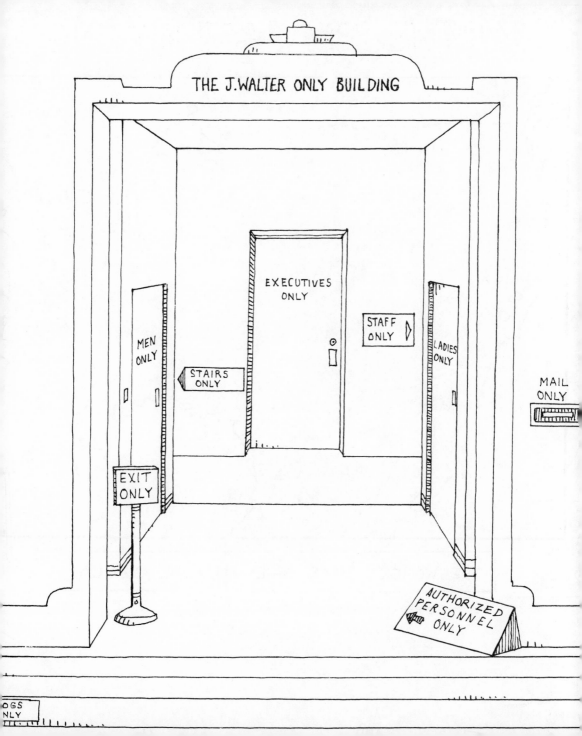

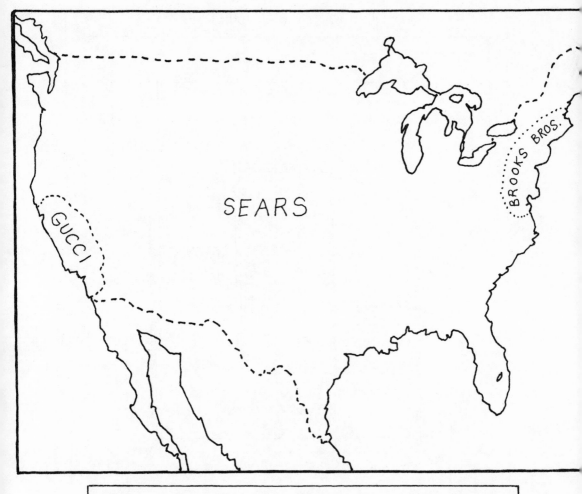

GUCCI

SEARS

BROOKS BROS.

THE WOMEN'S WEAR DAILY MAP OF AMERICA

YOU ARE NOW ENTERING

LAS VEGAS

PLEASE LEAVE YOUR GOOD TASTE
AT THE FRONT DESK

THE PRESIDENT
EATS OUT

'One burger and eight fries to go.'

SPRING TRAINING
ON A RAINY DAY

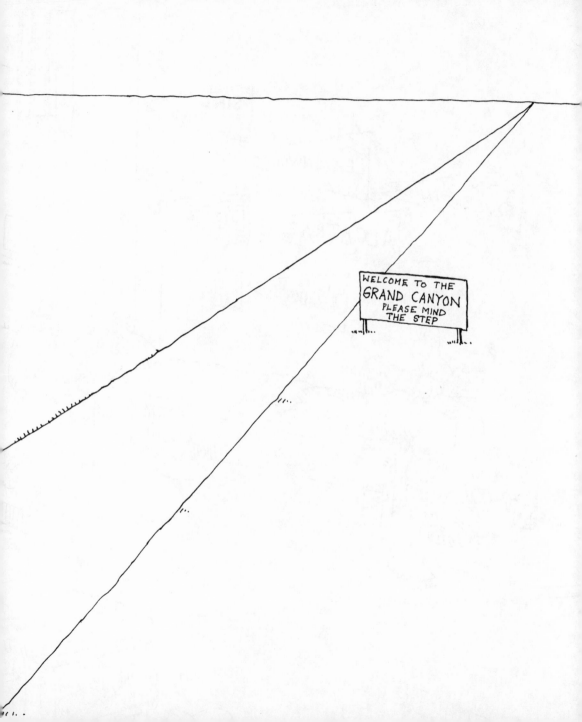

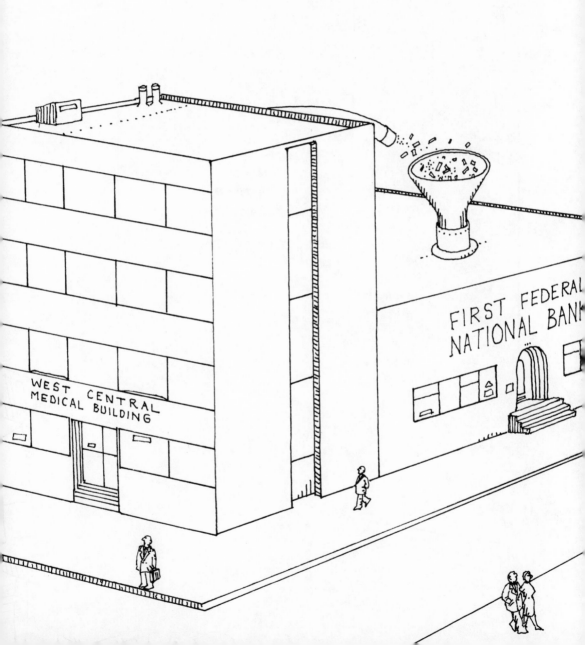

KENNEDY AIRPORT

PLANES DEPARTING	PLANES ARRIVING	PLANES PASSING BY	PLANES NOWHERE NEAR HERE
PA 109 LONDON	TWA 10 PARIS	A. MEXICO 70 MEXICO C.	AERO ACME DUBLIN
BA 64 M'CHESTER	AIR FR. 792 PARIS	AEROFLOT 88 WARSAW	ACE AIR 99 PHX. AZ.
TWA 171 ROME	SAB 10M BRUSSELS	B. CAL 680 GLASGOW	WIZZO AIR 6 NEWARK N.J.
PA 400 MADRID	EL AL 266 TEL AVIV	EASTERN 18 DALLAS	EL TORRO 60 S. DIEGO
LUF. 800 BERLIN	BA 68 BAHRAIN	WEST 604 SAN FRAN	CROPDUST 16 KANSAS
	AIR CANADA LONDON		

'Eight guilty, three not guilty
and one pepperoni pizza with extra cheese.'

'I'll be home a little late honey . . . I'm meeting with my lawyers!'

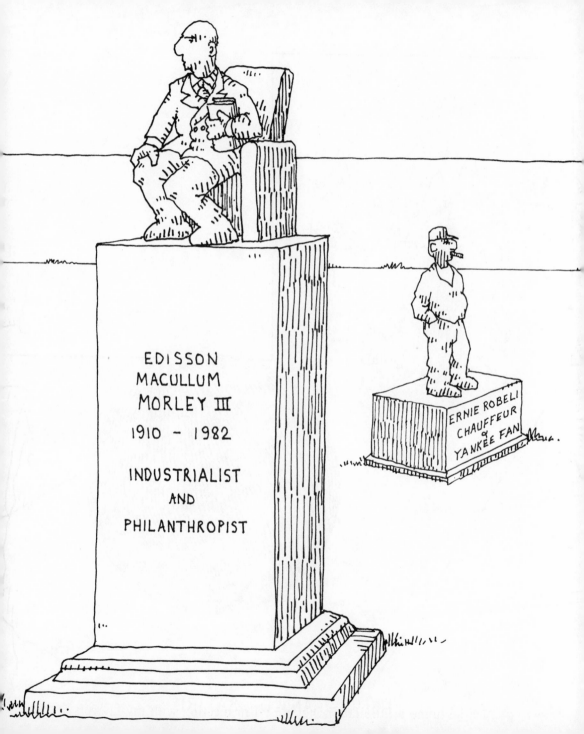

EDISSON
MACULLUM
MORLEY III

1910 – 1982

INDUSTRIALIST
AND
PHILANTHROPIST

ERNIE ROBELI
CHAUFFEUR
&
YANKEE FAN

HEAVY-HANDED SATIRE

MARTHA'S VINEYARD

MARTHA'S DRUNK

WHY WE HAVE ARCHITECTS

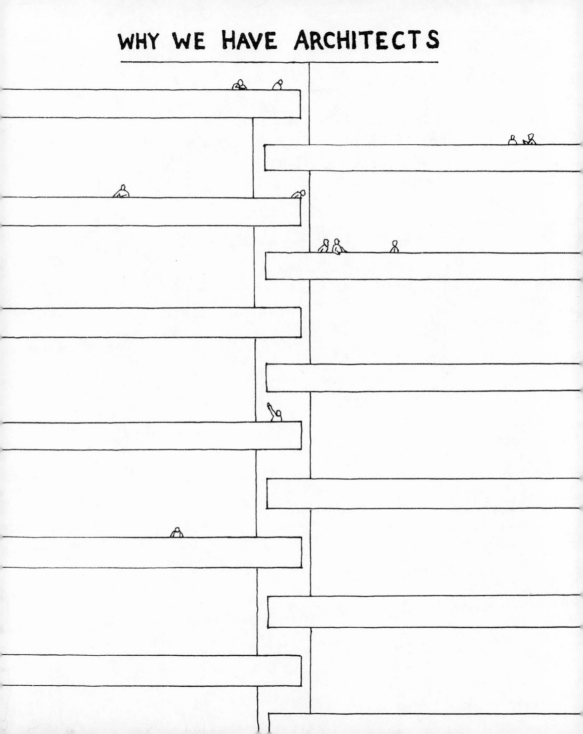

THE STATE OF THE NATION

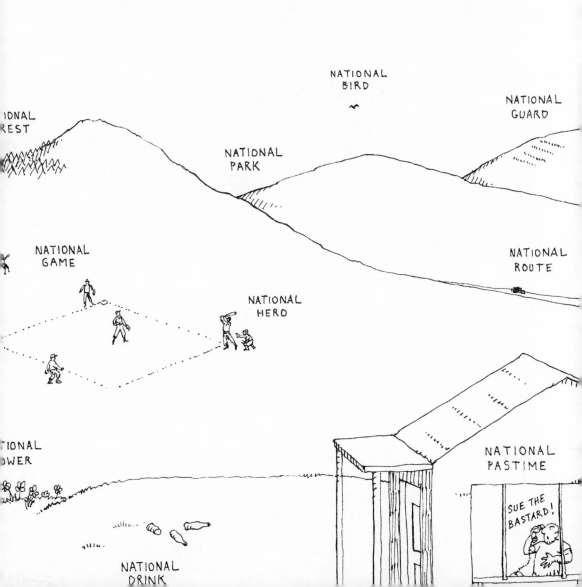

NATIONAL
BIRD

NATIONAL
GUARD

...IONAL
...REST

NATIONAL
PARK

NATIONAL
GAME

NATIONAL
ROUTE

NATIONAL
HERO

...TIONAL
...OWER

NATIONAL
PASTIME

SUE THE
BASTARD!

NATIONAL
DRINK

THE OUTSKIRTS OF WASHINGTON D.C.

WELCOME TO SEQUEETA COUNTY
ALL WELCOME
EXCEPT
BLACKS
JEWS
COMMIES
HIPPIES
MEXICANS
YANKIES
AND
LIBERALS
LIBBERS
CATHOLICS
OR
HOMOS
PLUS ANYONE WITH A THREE FIGURE I.Q.

'. . . and then you take a left at the First Church of Christ the
Redeemer . . . another left at the Everlasting Baptist Chapel . . .
second right at the Neverending Chapel of God the Giver . . .
straight past the Holy House of God the Good . . . another right at
the Trinity Church of the Secular Servant . . . left at the Metro
Miracle Mid-Town Tabernacle . . .'

A NEW CASH CROP FOR ALABAMA

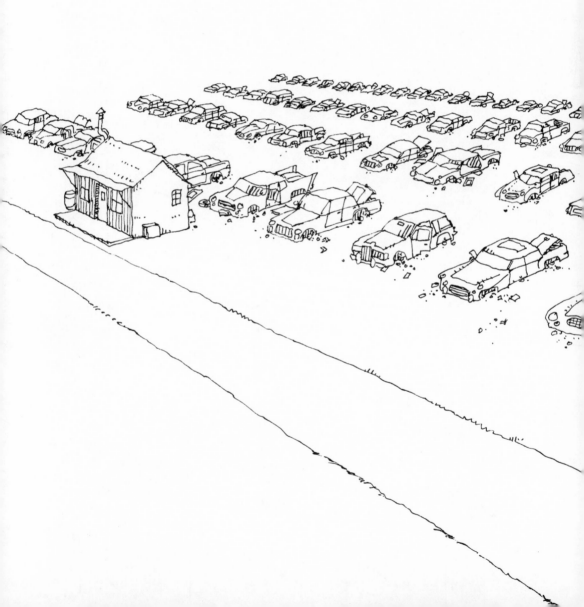

'It's rather a crude system but the customers seem to like it.'

'I'd like to buy a book on chutzpah
and I'd like you to pay for it.'

'I loved the book and the mini-series,
but I wasn't so keen on the record or the movie,
although the stage version and video were okay.'

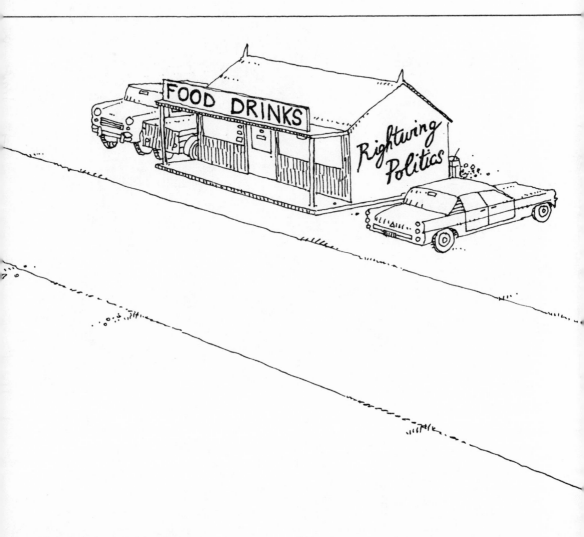

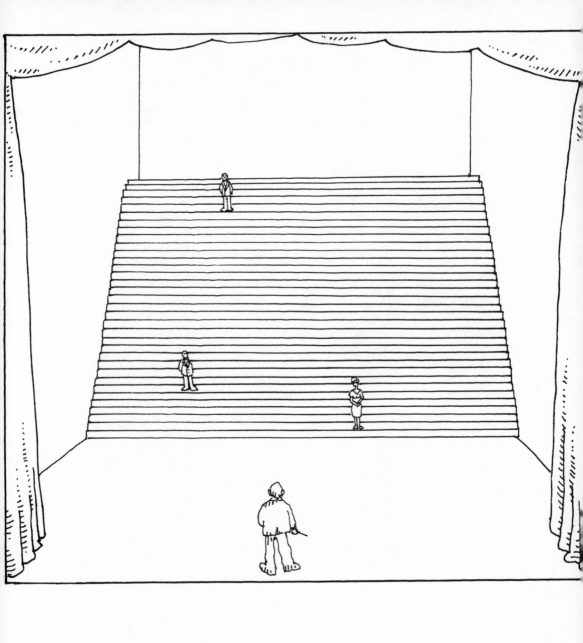

THE MORMON TABERNACLE TRIO

A CONGRESSIONAL HEARING

SUNDAY IN THE PARK

'Apparently I'm from New Heidelberg Springs, South Dakota
. . . but just where the hell is that?'

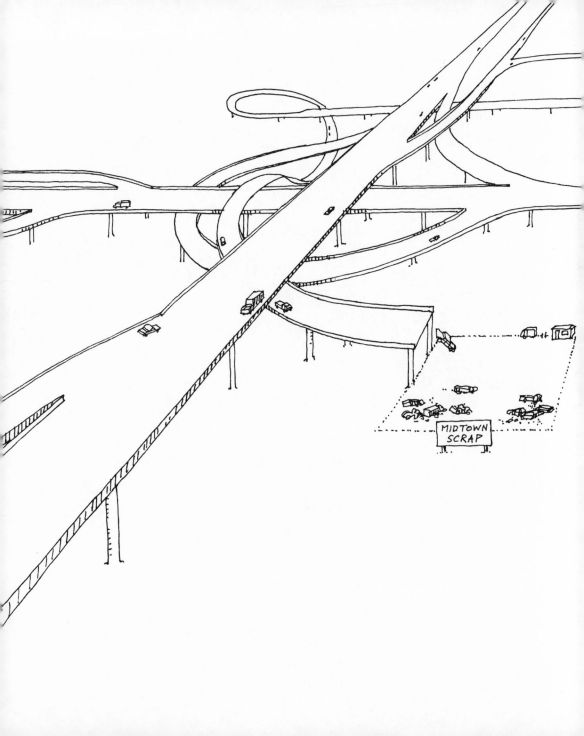

THE CONVERSATION FLAGGED
AFTER DELWOOD DIED

GOD BLESS AMERICA
THE LAND OF THE FREE & HOME OF THE BRAVE

WHY THE CAR WAS INVENTED

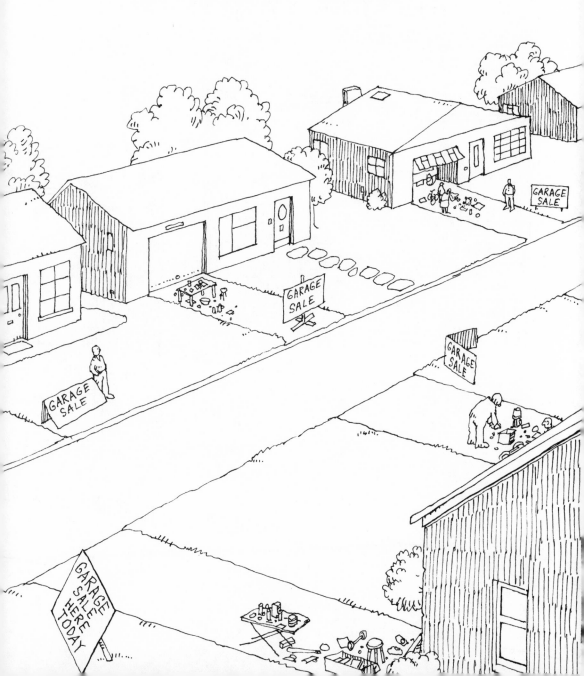

JAQUES
FRISSON
HIS PIANO
HIS SONGS

HIS PIPE
AND
HIS SLIPPERS

1176

CAFÉ LE MON

UN-AMERICAN ACTIVITIES

'More tea, dear?'

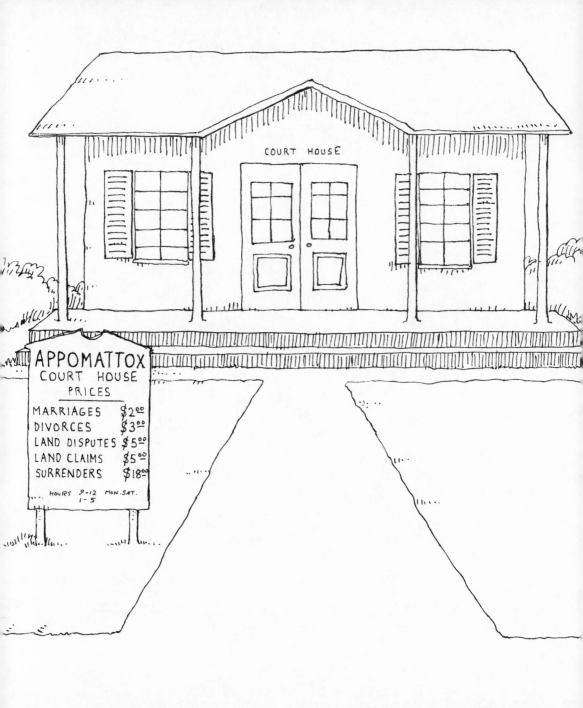

'Oh my God, the Apache Nation Marching Band!'

A CORRIDOR OF POWER

WASHINGTON D.C.

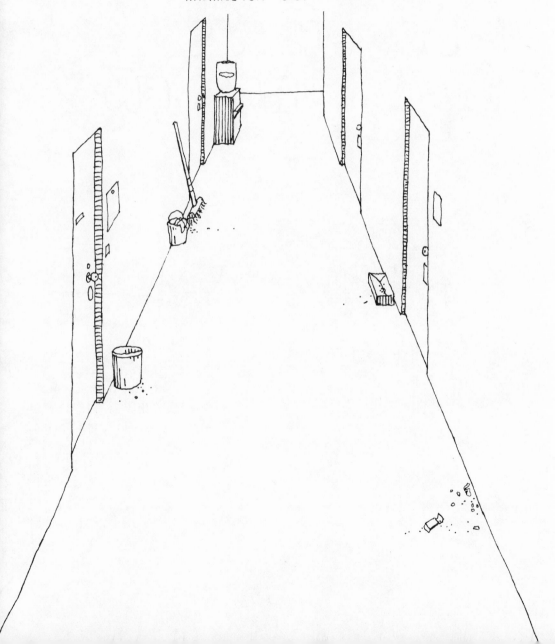

DOUGHNUT HEAVEN

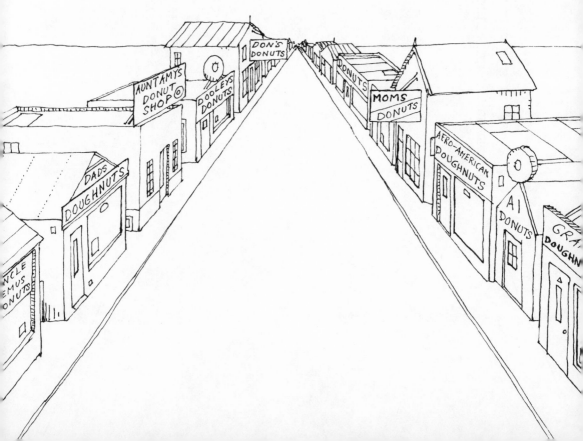

UNEXPECTED AMERICANS—*The Liberal Trucker.*

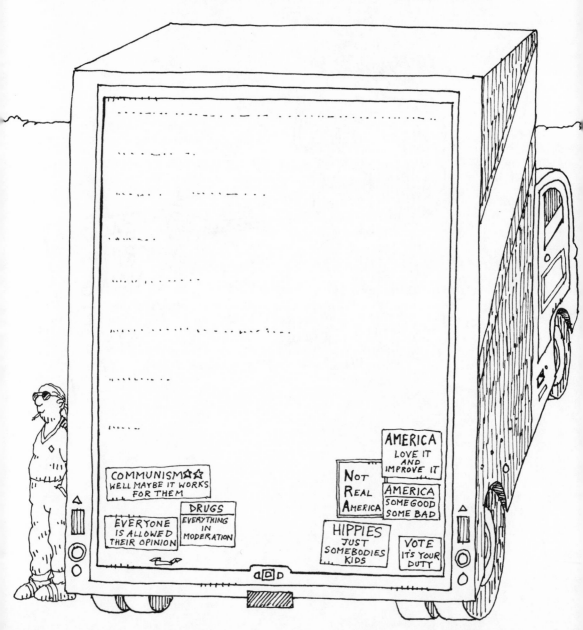

BORN AGAIN BUMS
ISN'T LIFE GREAT
HAVE A NICE DAY
PLEASE TAKE ONE
PLEASE ACCEPT THIS GIFT
GOD BLESS YOU

'Looks like trouble, Sheriff.'

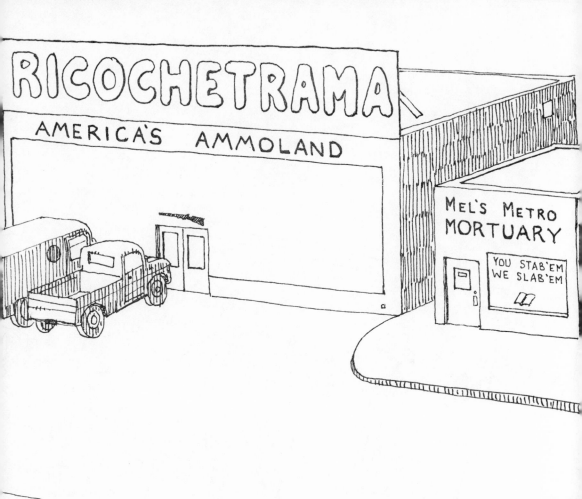

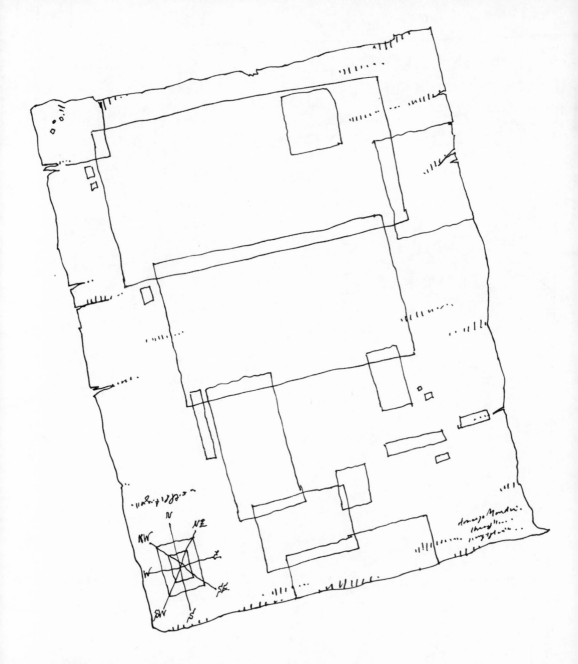

Amerigo Mondrian Discovers America 1491

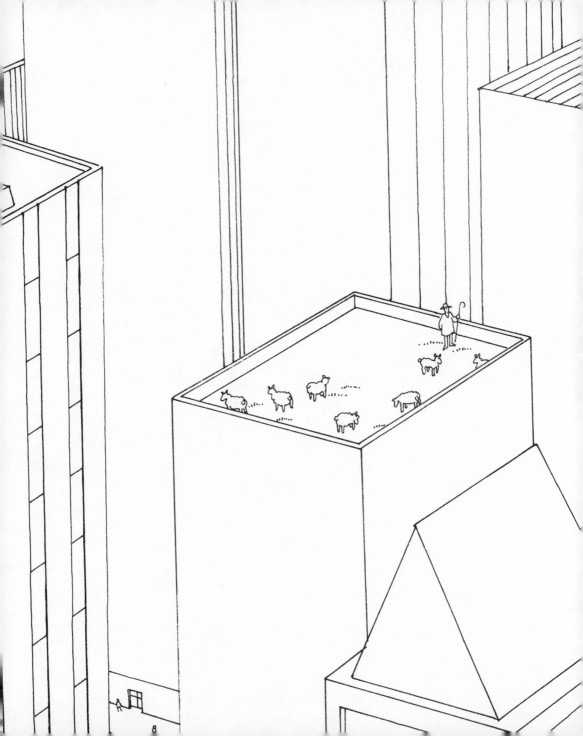

DIPLOMACY IN ACTION

'Listen Buddy, you'd better become a Democracy
by Thursday or we'll bomb the shit out of you!'

THE CINCINNATI BENGALS FORMATION DANCE TEAM

'I love it . . . but lose the bodies.'

'Thank you Lord for everything and by the way there's no more
tax on any of this is there?'

◯ JUPITER

◯ VENUS

◯ MARS

EARTH

CALIFORNIA

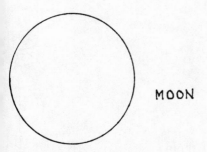

MOON

'It's all right . . . there's a lot of them,
but they've all surrendered.'

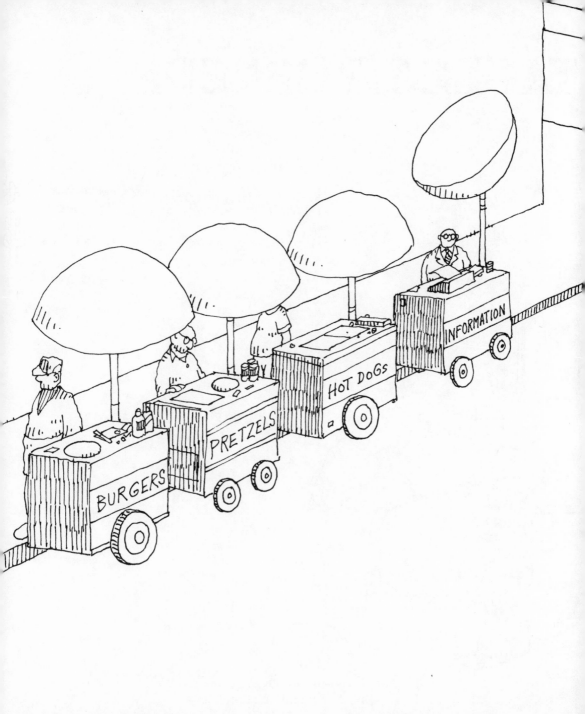

TABLES TURNED?

Hello, I'm Jeff... I'm your customer today... we'd both like mineral water to start, and a menu. My particular special is coq au vin and we will not be needing a wine list. We certainly hope to enjoy our meal   and should we need anything, we'll   certainly let you know.

PENNY CANDY
BOTTLED MILK
THE BROOKLYN DODGERS
RIP
HOWDY DOODY
STUDEBAKER
BURMA SHAVE
5¢ CIGAR

FINALLY AN HONEST MAN

'. . . and I promise to lie and cheat and line my pockets at each and every opportunity.'

AND ON THE EIGHTH DAY GOD MADE AMERICA

'Oh well, it'll have to do.'